The Dark Side of Destiny

The Dark Side of Destiny

Hell Re-Examined

J. Gregory Crofford

With a foreword
Edward William Fudge

WIPF & STOCK · Eugene, Oregon

THE DARK SIDE OF DESTINY
Hell Re-Examined

Wipf & Stock
An Imprint of Wipf and Stock Publishers
199 W. 8th Ave., Suite 3
Eugene, OR 97401

www.wipfandstock.com

ISBN 13: 978-1-62564-281-3

Manufactured in the U.S.A.

To Dr Paul Orjala, late Professor of Missiology
at Nazarene Theological Seminary,
who by his life modeled for his students that love
will always be the Christian impetus for missions

Contents

About the Author

J. GREGORY CROFFORD is the Education and Clergy Development Coordinator for the Africa Region of the Church of the Nazarene. He received his BA in religion from Eastern Nazarene College, his MDiv in missiology from Nazarene Theological Seminary, and his MA and PhD in theology from the University of Manchester, England. He has served cross-cultural assignments in Côte d'Ivoire, Benin, Haiti, Kenya, and South Africa, working in ministerial education and church planting. Dr. Crofford has also taught as an adjunct instructor in missions, Bible, and theology at several universities in the United States. Prior to missionary service, he pastored in Sedalia, Missouri. Crofford is an ordained elder in the Church of the Nazarene.

Dr. Crofford's other publications include *Streams of Mercy: Prevenient Grace in the Theology of John and Charles Wesley* (2010) and several articles in the *Global Wesleyan Dictionary of Theology* (2013).

Foreword

Three centuries ago, John Wesley preached a Hell of everlasting conscious torment as eloquently as his Calvinistic counterpart Jonathan Edwards ever did. But if Wesley were alive today, he would urge his spiritual descendants to test his ideas on Hell by Scripture, reason, tradition, and experience, and to evaluate the final three by the Bible, which always comes first.

Does God really intend to keep billions of people alive forever just to watch them writhe in neverending agony? How does such an idea measure up to Wesley's quadrilateral (four-part test)? To help fellow Wesleyans in particular find out, Nazarene missionary, professor, and pastor Dr. Gregory Crofford has written this handy little introduction to the ongoing debate on Hell. Those favoring unending conscious torment clearly have tradition on their side. But tradition is only one of four tests in Wesley's quadrilateral.

Dr. Crofford first looks at reason. The punishment must fit the crime—the principle of "proportionality." God is holy and God is love. How does unending torment look in light of those criteria? And what can we learn from experience? Does the traditional understanding of Hell enhance evangelism or does it hinder? The subject of Hell is joined to the character of God, and also to the nature of human beings.

In the end, Dr. Crofford recommends an alternative picture of final punishment known as "conditional immortality." He commends this view as thoroughly scriptural, very reasonable, and a view that works in the real world. It provides punishment that precisely fits the crime. It matches our nature and God's character. It encourages evangelism. It fits everything that Scripture says about Hell. What more could anyone—including John Wesley himself—honestly want?

Edward William Fudge

Prologue

Few ideas make people squirm more than Hell. Depending upon the spirit of the times, Hell has been either a club for preachers to beat listeners over the head, or the crazy aunt in the attic no one dares mention.

Rob Bell's *Love Wins* has people thinking about Hell. Bell questions the idea that God will punish evil-doers forever, hinting at a far more positive outcome. Bell's ideas have proven to be like gazing at clouds floating overhead—different people see different things. The former pastor's poetic but ambiguous language has some branding him a heretic, others singing his praises. While Bell dances deftly around the edges of universalism—the idea that all will eventually be admitted to God's eternal kingdom—he is silent about an alternative that rings truer with the whole message of the Bible. That position, one gaining ground among Christian thinkers, is championed in the closing chapters of this book.

Before any plant can thrive, weeds that would choke it must be uprooted. After presenting the problem of Hell, *The Dark Side of Destiny* examines various views on divine punishment in the afterlife. One by one, they are found wanting. By going back to the Bible and taking a fresh look, we discover a better understanding of Hell, one that is truer to God's character of loving holiness, a portrait of God painted by the broad sweep of Holy Scripture.

Paul writes: "I want to know Christ and the power of his resurrection and the fellowship of sharing in his sufferings, becoming like him in his death, and so, somehow, to attain to the resurrection of the dead" (Phil 3:11–12). Serving God is about much more than avoiding Hell or inheriting the kingdom of Heaven, as important as those are. Knowing Christ is about holiness, an ever-deepening love for God and others in *this* life. Unfortunately, well-intentioned but mistaken notions regarding the nature of future punishment and God's role in it keep too many believers from embracing a close relationship with a seemingly sadistic God. Wrong ideas, however longstanding, discourage profound love between us and God, undermining a better foundation for righteous living than fear alone could ever provide. By re-examining and, where necessary, correcting our thinking, we will discard erroneous ideas about human destiny, allowing for deeper intimacy with our Creator.

This book is short by design; chapters can be read in one sitting. Discussion questions follow, making the book ideal for a half-hour Sunday School session, a Bible study, or small group. Students interested in going deeper should consult the "For Further Reading" section at the back of the book.

Appreciation is due Clark Pinnock (now awaiting the final trumpet call) and Edward Fudge, two scholars who opened my eyes to biblical truths previously overlooked. Mr. Fudge penned the Foreword and suggested improvements, a kindness for which I am indebted. I am also grateful to James Copple, Carol Rotz, John Crofford,

James Brown, Stephen Doan, and Brad Crofford, who read and critiqued the first draft. Amy Crofford, my wife, has been a faithful sounding board, helping fine-tune concepts. While this book is better because of them, any final imperfections are mine alone. If these pages shed any light on a dark topic, my mission will have been accomplished.

J. Gregory Crofford
Johannesburg, South Africa
September 2013

1

The God of Fair Play

The infliction of cruelty with a good conscience is
a delight to moralists. That is why they invented Hell.
—Bertrand Russell

Do you like reading comment threads on news web-
sites? It's one of my favorite things to do. I've noticed
that when one of the "hot button" topics is in the news,
a nasty argument can ensue. Inevitably, a Christian will
write: "That's a sin, and if they don't repent, they'll go to
Hell." Often, others respond that they could "never believe in a God that would allow someone to be tormented
forever in Hell."

If this last response was rare, I might discount it. But
it's there, *over and over again.* Because I've been raised
in the community of faith, I find it difficult to look at
Christianity through the eyes of a person on the "outside."
Yet there they are, not just an isolated few, but many who
are saying: "Look, if that's what God is like, who needs
God?"

1

What is going on here? God has placed in the human heart a notion of fair play. When children sense that they or their friends are being mistreated, they often protest: "That's not fair!" We grow up and learn that *life* isn't always fair because *people* aren't always fair, but we still expect more from the God of the Bible.

Abraham asked the Lord as he pleaded for him to spare two towns: *"Will not the Judge of all the earth do right?"* (Gen 18:25). Yes, God will, and not only will God do what is right, God expects us to do the same. That is the basis of the *lex talionis*, the law of retaliation. This is the famous "eye for an eye" precept in Exodus 21:24. Kevin Vanhoozer notes that this law "limits revenge and takes the first step toward leaving revenge to God and ultimately to forgiving one's enemies."[1] But by Jesus' time, his fellow Jews had totally missed this lesson of proportionate response, of having the "punishment fit the crime," so Christ modified the precept, telling the offended to swear off retaliation of any sort, to instead "turn the other cheek" (Matt 5:38–39). In short, even-handed retribution is so important that it would be better not to retaliate at all than to respond disproportionately to an offense.

So here we have a snapshot of one aspect of God's character. While God punishes sin (Rom 6:23), the "Judge of all the earth" does so in an equitable manner, modeling the principle of *lex talionis*, of proportionate judgment. For God to refuse to follow God's own law would be like the parent who says to her child: "Do what I say, and not what I do." If a child would not respect such a double standard in a parent, why should a worshiper overlook it in the divine-human relationship?

1. Vanhoozer, *Theological Interpretation of the Old Testament*, 56.

Yet many envision Hell as a place where individuals are punished forever. They are awake and aware of their torment, and will be for all eternity. Hell as unending, conscious torment is precisely where objections arise. How so? The human lifespan averages from fifty years (in African countries) to more than seventy years in the Western world. Let's consider the most despicable person possible, perhaps Pol Pot, the Cambodian butcher, or Josef Stalin, the Russian dictator responsible for the deaths of millions of Russians. For such heinous crimes, the concept of unending torment may be acceptable, but let's face it: *Most cases are not so clear*. The vast majority of those who have lived on this earth have never murdered another person, though Paul correctly notes that all have sinned (Rom 3:23). When pressed, many would admit to other offenses, such as shoplifting, cheating on a test at school, or perhaps having been unfaithful in marriage. No, these are not to be brushed off lightly, but who is willing to argue that these reach the same level as dictators who presided over genocide? Yet the traditional doctrine of Hell consigns one and all to the same dark destiny. If the *lex talionis* means proportionate punishment, then for most, the punishment is infinitely greater than the crime. For one lifetime rejecting God, as regrettable as that is, God consigns an individual to a hellish existence that *never ends*. And so those curious about the Christian faith look on and conclude: "That's not fair. If that's how God is, count me out."

Suppose that you are distracted behind the wheel of your car. You know you shouldn't, but you do it anyways: You send that text message, then looking up too late, you slam into the car in front of you. Thankfully, no one is injured, but your car and theirs are seriously damaged and must be towed away. The police arrive on the scene and ticket you. "Don't you know that it's illegal to text while driving?" the officer asks. "Your court date is August 10. Be there at 9 a.m."

Meanwhile, in the same city, a rapist breaks into a home, violates the female homeowner, then slashes her throat. She is the fifteenth victim of this serial killer, a brutal psychopath who has struck terror in the hearts of the population. Later that evening, a patrolman stops a car because its taillight is out. When he approaches the driver, he recognizes the killer and calls for back up. Ten minutes later, the monster is in custody. His sentencing is set for August 10 at 9 a.m.

August 10 comes. Both you and the serial killer arrive in the courtroom. You, the careless texter, are smarter this time and leave your cell phone at home, driving to the courthouse in your repaired vehicle. As for the murderer, he is closely guarded and wears orange prison clothes and ankle chains. His trial has already happened, a jury having found him guilty on all counts. The judge orders him to stand, then dramatically reads the sentence: "I sentence you to life in prison, with no chance of parole."

Now it is your turn. You rise, and the judge asks you: "How do you plead?" Embarrassed, you reply: "Guilty." The judge looks down at you, then pronounces judgment: "I sentence you to life in prison, with no chance of parole."

"That could never happen!" you say. "That would be a total miscarriage of justice," yet that is exactly what the traditional view of Hell claims. It is endless separation from God, unending, conscious punishment for all who reject God during their lifetime, no matter the nature of their offenses. *Is that what the Christian God is like?*

There are some who will object: "The idea of 'fairness' cannot exist apart from God. If God does it, by definition, it is fair." Yet is this not merely projecting onto heaven the morally bankrupt notion of "might makes right"? We look at the old legends of the Greek gods and their lack of holiness, their capricious cavorting and their frequent disrespect of any notion of decency, and we say: "They're no better than humans!" It was precisely because of the ancient gods' moral failings that Christianity with its rigorous ethical standards appealed so strongly to those living in the first centuries AD. We must be very careful not to borrow unworthy character traits from the pagan gods and overlay them onto the portrait of our loving and holy God.

Divine judgment is a biblical doctrine, but the question remains: *Does the traditional concept of Hell compute with what we know about the character of God?* Or could it be that we have placed in front of non-believers a huge stumbling block to faith, a needless obstacle incompatible with the God of the *lex talionis* or the Jesus of Matthew 5:38–39? To this issue and others we turn in the next chapter.

For discussion

1. When someone uses the word "Hell," what comes to mind for you? What are some of the popular ways in which Hell has been conceived? How does routinely using the words "hell" and "damn" as filler words in our vocabulary affect the conversation about Hell?

2. The author cites instances where non-believers—in light of Hell—question the nature of God. Have you had similar conversations with others? If so, share them with the group. Do you agree that Hell as traditionally taught can be an obstacle to faith? Why or why not?

3. Debate whether it is legitimate to cite the Old Testament principle of *lex talionis* in the discussion regarding the concept of Hell as unending, conscious torment. How would you respond to someone who says that using this argument is dangerous since it allows us as mere humans to judge God?

4. Review what you've read of Greek and Roman mythology, then make a list of the divine characteristics of the gods. (If you know about other deities, such as ones worshipped in Africa or Asia, you could describe those instead). Next, make another list of God's attributes, as presented in the Bible. How are they similar? How are they different? Which ones apply to the discussion of Hell?

2

Our Loving and Holy God

Holiness has love for its essence,
humility for its clothing,
the good of others as its employment,
and the honor of God as its end.

—Nathanael Emmons

Though my brothers and I growing up were far from perfect, we avoided the trap of smoking. This was likely because neither of our parents smoked cigarettes. One Sunday morning came, and—as usual—we went to church. Before Sunday school, my father hunted some chalk for the chalkboard in his classroom. Since his hands were already full with a Bible and lesson books, he slipped the stick of white chalk between his lips, heading down the corridor. Suddenly, my younger brother, only five at the time, poked his head into the hallway. He glanced up, and with a look of surprise on his face exclaimed: "Daddy, I didn't know that you smoke!"

My little brother was surprised at what he saw because it seemed totally out of character. After all, he had never seen his dad smoke before, so why was he starting now? It didn't fit what he knew about our father, knowledge gained over time through first-hand experience.

Just like my brother knew that our father smoking didn't fit what he knew of his dad, so God endlessly punishing the wrongdoer doesn't fit what we know about God's character. Chapter 1 considered the *lex talionis* as related to the popular idea of Hell as unending, conscious torment. We were reminded that one aspect of our heavenly Father's character is even-handedness. God is fair when dealing with offenders. Because God models this trait, he expects the same proportionality in our relationships. An "eye for an eye, and a tooth for a tooth" (Exod 21:24) is not an excuse to obliterate our enemies, but a call for reasonable and measured response when addressing wrongs. Because the concept of Hell as unending, conscious torment fails the test of *lex talionis*, we have reason to call it into question. But *what else do we know about the character of God?*

Kenneth Collins described God's character as "holy love."[2] We could just as well speak of God's "loving holiness." No priority is implied in the order of the words; they are equally true. God's love for us is a consistent New Testament teaching. John wrote: "For God so loved the world, that he gave his only Son . . ." (John 3:16a, NLT). Paul joined John in his appraisal, extolling the virtue of God, who "showed his great love for us by sending Christ to die for us while we were still sinners" (Rom 5:8, NLT).

2. Collins, *Theology of John Wesley,* 20–22.

Jesus said: "Anyone who has seen me has seen the Father" (John 14:9, TNIV). In the face of Christ, we see the love of God the Father, a love that sent the prophet Jonah on a mission to Nineveh, all because of God's great concern for the people of that city (Jonah 4:11).

Yet as important as love is to the character of God, it is not all that the Bible has to say. God is loving, but God is also holy. Holiness refers to God's moral purity or goodness. "God is light," said John, "and there is no darkness in him at all" (1 John 1:5). All that is "good" and "perfect" is a reflection of the character of God (Jas 1:17). Because God is holy, he asks us to be holy, and empowers us to live a righteous life (1 Pet 1:16). The mandate to live an upright life includes God's willingness to punish disobedience (Acts 5:1–11). While this may seem to contradict God's loving nature, on further reflection, it is an eloquent demonstration of divine love. By disciplining us, God treats us as his children (Heb 12:5–11). What is true now will also be true in the future. One day, the Son will judge the world with "justice" (Acts 17:31). We will all stand before Christ to be judged (2 Cor 5:10). The equitable judgment of God is a corollary of his holiness. This is hardly a case of "do what I say and not what I do." Because God is holy in character and conduct, God is justified as Creator in judging the creation.

So far we have considered two important statements about God's character. God is love and God is holy. One attribute does not "trump" the other. The key is to keep them in balance. Finding the "middle way" can be easier said than done. In Nairobi, Kenya, the rainy season can wreak havoc on the lightly paved roads. Often, both sides of the road will wash out. Traffic backs up in both directions as cars take turns navigating the narrow asphalt section in the middle. Patience is a must, or else you might end up in the ditch on either side!

As with driving, so it is with understanding God's character. Place an exclusive emphasis upon God's love and you'll end up in the ditch on the right. Conversely, talk only about the holiness of God and you'll fall into the ditch on the left. In all discussion of the divine—including our discussion of Hell—to stay out of the "ditches," we must maintain the creative tension of God as both loving and holy.

Conclusion

Whatever Hell is, it must be consistent with what we know of God. First, as we saw in chapter 1, it must respond to divine even-handedness, the proportional law of retaliation (*lex talionis*) that God models for us. Secondly, it must not violate the law of love, a love that does all that it possibly can to save us. Finally, it cannot disregard sin or treat it as unimportant, since God is by very nature holy. Our Father of light offers us his hand, leading us—if we allow him—out of the darkness of evil into God's incredible light. In chapter 3, we'll discuss the traditional doctrine of Hell as unending, conscious punishment. The objective will be to answer this question: *Does this idea fit with what we know about God's character?* But before we turn the page, let's discuss what we've learned in this chapter.

For Discussion

1. Go back to the list of God's attributes that you made during the discussion at the end of chapter 1. Which attributes are closely related to God's love? What other divine characteristics could be categorized under God's holiness? Is your list balanced? Does this exercise support Ken Collins' contention that God's nature is best described as "holy love"?

2. Sometimes people consider the Old Testament God as severe, while the New Testament pictures a God of love. Take a few minutes to consider New Testament instances where God is severe and times in the Old Testament when God is loving. In light of your discussion, would you agree or disagree that the Bible speaks with a unified voice regarding God as "holy love"?

3. John Wesley (1703–91)—who with his brother, Charles, was the co-founder of Methodism—was known for being true to his Church of England heritage, promoting a *via media* (middle way) in Christian thought. How might the *via media* concept prove helpful as we examine what the Bible says about Hell?

3

Back On Your Heads!

I think Hell is a real place where
real people spend a real eternity.

—JERRY FALWELL

Mike Douglas, the 1970s talk show host, once told
a story of Hell. An evil man died, and his escort
led him down a long hall. Through the darkness, the man
could just make out on the left the shape of three doors.
The first door swung open, and the two stepped inside.
The room was huge, lined wall to wall with people standing on their heads as a demon sat to one side, enforcing
their punishment. "I'd like to look at the second room,
please" the man asked. The man and his escort exited,
walking down the hall to the second door. Inside, they
found the same thing, a room filled with people balanc-
ing awkwardly and painfully on their heads. "Is there
another option?" he asked his escort. Behind the third
door, the man found a different scene. A demon was still
there supervising but was seated, calmly drinking cof-

fee along with everyone in the room. "This doesn't seem too bad," the man mused out loud. "I choose this room." He stepped over to the coffee pot as the door swung closed and locked behind him. Suddenly, the demon announced: "OK everybody. Coffee break is over. Back on your heads!"

We chuckle at that kind of humor because we recognize it for what it is, an attempt to make light of a profoundly disturbing subject. Jonathan Edwards was an eighteenth-century New England cleric. Today, he is best known for his foreboding sermon, *Sinners in the Hands of an Angry God*. In this 1741 homily, Edwards pictured God as one who dangles the sinner over the pit of Hell, like a spider over an open flame. Here, the torment of Hell is not for a time, but unending:

> There will be no end to this extreme horrible misery. When you look forward, you shall see a long forever, a boundless duration before you, which will swallow up your thoughts, and amaze your soul; and you will absolutely despair of ever having any deliverance, any end, any mitigation, any rest at all. You will know certainly that you must wear out long ages, millions of millions of ages in wrestling and conflicting with this almighty merciless vengeance; and then when you have so done, when so many ages have actually been spent by you in this manner, you will know that all is but a point to what remains. So that your punishment will indeed be infinite.[1]

Edwards was not alone in his dreadful doctrine of Hell as unending, conscious torment. He merely pictured in more vivid terms what had already been affirmed in

1. Edwards, *Sinners in the Hands of an Angry God.*

historic creeds. The *Westminster Confession of Faith* (1646) taught in its thirty-second chapter that—following final judgment—the "wicked," those "who know not God," shall be "cast into eternal torments, and be punished with everlasting destruction from the presence of the Lord, and from the glory of His power."[2] John Calvin, the sixteenth century Geneva pastor, described the terrors of Hell for the damned:

> Consequently, unhappy consciences find no rest from being troubled and tossed by a terrible whirlwind, from feeling that they are being torn asunder by a hostile Deity, pierced and lanced by deadly darts, quaking at God's lightning bolt, and being crushed by the weight of his hand, so that it would be more bearable to go down into any bottomless depths and chasms than to stand for a moment in these terrors. What and how great is this, to be eternally and unceasingly besieged by him?[3]

John Walvoord—following in the broad Calvinistic tradition—called eternal punishment an "unrelenting doctrine that faces every human being as the alternative to grace and salvation in Jesus Christ."[4] Walvoord's position is representative of the North American twentieth century evangelical consensus.

In eighteenth century England, John Wesley also preached about a place of "torment" that is "without end" in the "lake of fire, burning with brimstone."[5] The

2. *Westminster Confession of Faith*, ch. 33, "Of the Last Judgment."

3. McNeill, ed., *Calvin: Institutes*, 2:1008.

4. In Crockett, ed., *Four Views on Hell*, 28.

5. From Wesley's 1775 sermon *The Important Question*, in Baker, ed., *Works of John Wesley*, 3:188.

Church of the Nazarene, a denomination in the Wesleyan tradition, teaches that "the finally impenitent shall suffer eternally in hell."[6] Orton Wiley, a leading Nazarene theologian, likewise affirmed: "The general judgment not only makes possible the bestowment of eternal blessedness upon the saints, but necessitates also the sentence of endless punishment upon the finally impenitent and wicked."[7]

It is sobering to call into question the interpretation of a long line of thinkers. Nevertheless, the recent rejection by many of the traditional view of Hell at very least should encourage the church to check and double-check its conclusions. While our experience does not trump Scripture, it forces us to be very sure that we've gotten our interpretation correct.

To reassess the traditional interpretation of Hell, let us return to the three elements of God's character addressed in chapters 1–2. Looking at Scripture, we established that:

1. *God models the principle of proportionality in punishment.* Exodus 21:24, the *lex talionis,* called Israel to punish the wrongdoer in the proper measure. The punishment must fit the crime. Jesus in Matthew 5:38–39 appeared to be responding to a misapplication of this principle, which many took to be divine approval of vengeance without boundaries. Because of this, Jesus encouraged the offended to "turn the other cheek," a reminder that it is better to forgive than to risk the excess of revenge.

6. Article of Faith 16, "Resurrection, Judgment, and Destiny," in *Manual of the Church of the Nazarene,* 36.

7. Wiley and Culbertson, *Introduction to Christian Theology,* 435.

2. *God is love.* This is one emphasis of the New Testament witness as epitomized in the life of Christ. As the perfect reflection of the character of the Father, Jesus showed a love greater than all, laying down his life for his friends (John 15:13). How Jesus *acts* is how God *is* since Jesus himself said: "He who has seen me has seen the Father" (John 14:9, NASB).

3. *God is holy.* As the One who is good and just, God calls us to the same standard (1 Pet 1:16). Because God enables us to be holy, he will correct his own (Heb 12:5–11). A holy Creator expects obedience from his creation, and has fixed a final day of judgment (Acts 17:31, 2 Cor 5:10).

Using these three elements of God's character as a benchmark, how does the traditional concept of Hell as unending, conscious torment, fare? The third element, God's holiness, is vindicated. God cannot brush aside sin, and divine willingness to punish individuals in Hell underscores the serious nature of sin. However, the first and second items on the list appear to be violated. If the "punishment must fit the crime" in our human interactions, according to the principle God has given humanity, then must not God also be subject to the same criterion? Yet assigning an individual to *endless* torment for crimes committed over a period of *decades* exceeds all bounds. Such a fate is in glaring contradiction to the character of God as we have come to know it in the face of Jesus Christ.

Most importantly, in the traditional view of Hell, the law of love is nowhere to be seen. The Old Testament book of Hosea presents a God who has been wronged by Israel, yet unfailingly loves his wife, wanting her to return and be faithful. He is the God who "takes no pleasure in the death of the wicked" (Ezek 18:23). Our God is a God of *hesed*, the Hebrew word for unfailing love. God is willing to punish a family to the "third and fourth generation" yet shows love to "a thousand generations of those who love me and keep my commandments" (Exod 20:5–6). Yes, God will measure out reasonable punishment, but punishment is always tempered by love, seeking redemption.

When approaching specific passages of the Bible, we must remember to relate them to the teaching of Scripture as a whole. This is called the "analogy of faith." John Wesley taught that the interpretation of a given verse(s) must not contradict the general sense of the whole of Scripture.[8] Through the Bible's many parts, an overall picture of God's character emerges. If our conclusion from a text of Scripture does not resemble that portrait, then we need to go back and study the passage again. This will be an important principle to respect as our study progresses.

Conclusion

This chapter has approached the traditional doctrine of Hell from a theological perspective. It has not attempted to look at every passage that could be cited in its favor. Nonetheless, Hell as unending, conscious punishment fails the first two parts of the three-fold test of *lex talionis*, love, and holiness. Because of these shortcomings, we must find another alternative that arises out of a reason-

8. Oden, *John Wesley's Scriptural Christianity*, 57–58.

able interpretation of the Bible in its totality, but at the same time does justice to specific passages relevant to our topic. To this task we will turn in the following chapters.

For Discussion

1. Like the humorous story from Mike Douglas, there are many portrayals of Heaven and Hell in popular culture. Think of a recent movie, song or joke that talks about human destiny. What lesson does it teach? How does it compare with the truth of Scripture?

2. What do you think of the three-fold test of *lex talionis*, love and holiness? Are there any other benchmarks from Scripture that you would add?

3. When is it appropriate to call into question long-standing interpretations of Scripture? Can you think of any other issues addressed in the Bible where one view dominated for a long time but was eventually discarded? What are the potential benefits and dangers of re-evaluating long-held beliefs?

4. Explain the concept of the "analogy of faith" as taught by John Wesley. Why is it an important principle when evaluating what Scripture has to say about human destiny?

4

Are There Second Chances after Death?

If I have to spend time in purgatory
before going to one place or the other,
I guess I'll be alright as long as there's a lending library.
—STEPHEN KING

Many are the mistakes of a rookie teacher. The course syllabus had clearly given a due date. All of my students but one brought their completed project to class. When a less-than-conscientious student raised his hand and asked for an extension, I granted it on the spot, in front of everyone. Unfortunately, what I thought was a gracious act toward one student lost me the respect of many. After all, they were ready. Why wasn't he? By extending the deadline, I had unwittingly punished the preparedness of every other student.

God will act differently than rookie instructors, if we believe the teaching of Jesus. In the parable of the ten maidens (Matt 25:1–13), being ready at all times is the primary lesson, but the parable also teaches that there are no second chances. Among the maidens, five were wise and five were foolish. They all waited for the bridegroom's arrival. When the bridegroom delayed his coming, the five foolish maidens—who had brought no extra oil for their lamps—had to run off to buy more. While they were gone, the bridegroom suddenly arrived. The five wise maidens went into the marriage feast. The end of v. 10 gives pause: "And the door was shut." Later, the foolish maidens came back from their errand. "Sir! Sir!" they said. "Open the door open to us" (v. 11). Solemnly, the bridegroom replied: "I tell you the truth, I don't know you" (v. 12).

Whether at the second coming or at our own demise, we know that we will meet Christ, the bridegroom. We have time to prepare now, but there is coming a time when it will be too late. Like the maidens who were unprepared and found the door closed, too many today still procrastinate, foolishly delaying their preparation for that crucial rendezvous. Many want the bridegroom to announce: "I changed my mind. No problem, come on in!" These are well-intentioned people, individuals troubled by the view of Hell as unending, conscious torment, the majority position among Christians. This view affirms that those who refuse to forsake their sin and follow Christ during this life will be in agony, separated forever from God. (Review chapters 1–3 for a summary of the traditional conception and some of its difficulties.)

Historically, Hell as unending, conscious torment is not the only option. Some Christian thinkers have found it incompatible with the biblical portrait of God, especially the principles of fairness and justice. One way out of the dilemma is to make future punishment not final, but remedial. The two forms that this *post mortem* (after death) second chance viewpoint takes are *purgatory* and *universalism*. Let's look at both through the eyes of the three criteria laid down in previous chapters. Any position must take into account these elements of the character of God:

1. God will punish proportionately, the concept of *lex talionis* (Exod 21:23–25);

2. God is love;

3. God is holy.

After applying this test to purgatory and universalism, we will offer a brief analysis of relevant biblical texts, weighing the role of the human will—enabled by God's grace—in the equation.

Purgatory

What is "purgatory"? Zachary Hayes defined purgatory as the "state, place, or condition in the next world between heaven and hell, a state of purifying suffering for those who have died and are still in need of such purification."[9] The Catechism of the Roman Catholic Church speaks of purgatory as "purification, so as to achieve the holiness necessary to enter the joy of heaven." It is for those "who die in God's grace and friendship, but still imperfectly purified."[10] Furthermore, according to the purgatorial

9. In Crockett, ed., *Four Views on Hell*, 92.

10. Quoted from "Purgatory," online: http://www.catholic.com/tracts/purgatory.

view, others will be consigned to eternal punishment in Hell, "those who die in personal mortal sin, as enemies of God."[11]

Purgatory assumes the belief that after life on earth, but prior to the resurrection, there is an "intermediate state" of some sort. Many point to the parable of the rich man and Lazarus (Luke 16:19–31) as teaching this truth. However, N. T. Wright cautioned that to take this parable literally "is about as sensible as trying to find out the name of the Prodigal Son."[12] Jesus' story is a cautionary tale meant for this life and is not a road map to the next. It is a warning to the rich who callously neglect the needs of the poor. Nevertheless, the parable's evocative imagery has proven irresistible to those searching for details of life beyond the grave.

With the intermediate state allowed, speculation proceeded unabated. Pope Gregory the Great (AD 540–604) built upon earlier thinkers, more clearly describing a place where sins are purged *post mortem* (after death). Revelation 21:27 insists that nothing impure can enter heaven, so purgatory becomes a way to deal with lesser offenders, for "venial sins" or the "temporal punishment due to sins already forgiven."[13] Protestant denominations as well as Anglicanism and Methodism have rejected the doctrine of purgatory, citing a lack of biblical warrant. However, the Roman Catholic Bible includes 2 Maccabees 12:46, which speaks of praying for the dead, that "they may be loosed from sins" (v. 46).[14]

11. Hontheim, "Hell," in the section "Name and Place of Hell."
12. Wright, *Surprised by Hope*, 177.
13. Hontheim, "Hell," in the section "Name and Place of Hell."
14. See Hanna, "Purgatory."

Here, our three-fold test of proportional punishment, love, and holiness appears to support purgatory. Because the time spent in purgatory is of limited duration, it does not contradict the fairness of God. Secondly, the test of love is satisfied, since the punishment is remedial. Finally, the holiness of God and divine justice are maintained, because sin is taken seriously and must be atoned.

Yet there are other important considerations. Holiness is mandatory if we want to "see the Lord" (Heb 12:14b), but what is the time frame during which holiness must be acquired? The first part of verse 14 calls us to "live in peace," suggesting that the pursuit of peace and holiness is a here-and-now mandate. Accordingly, we must ask: *Does purgatory or any idea that promises second chances after death discourage obedience to God in the present?* As long as we think that we are guaranteed a second chance to make things right with God, we are likely to procrastinate, counting on that final opportunity. William Greathouse remarked that the popular *Left Behind* series of novels presents a Protestant version of purgatory.[15] Why live for Christ now if we can always join the "Trib Force" and fight the devil during the so-called Great Tribulation, thereby earning a spot in heaven? Likewise, the danger of the Roman Catholic doctrine of purgatory is that it may give false hope of a last chance to make things right.

Beyond the question of whether purgatory discourages righteous living, the greatest objection to the concept is its lack of support within the New Testament, a twenty-seven-book collection shared by Protestants and

15. From an email conversation with the author, 2002.

Catholics. Zachary Hayes cited 1 Corinthians 3:11–15 and the "fire" that will "test the quality of each person's work" (v. 13). He admitted, however, that this is more likely a reference to the final judgment.[16] Further, Hebrews 9:27 outlines the sequence as "death" and then "judgment." Though there may be an intermediate state, we have no indication anywhere in the New Testament that during this period there will be a second chance. Instead, as we saw above in the parable of the ten maidens (Matt 25:1–13), we must be ready in this life to meet the "bridegroom," who symbolizes Christ. A failure to be ready in the here-and-now means the door of opportunity will be shut at a later time.

John Wesley viewed the Scriptural basis of purgatory as deficient. His Twenty-Five Articles of Religion were adapted for American Methodism in 1784, abridged from the Thirty-Nine Articles of Religion of the Church of England. Wesley's Article 14, "Of Purgatory," affirmed: "The Romish doctrine concerning purgatory, pardon, worshiping, and adoration, as well of images of relics, and also invocation of saints, is a fond thing, vainly invented, and grounded upon no warrant of Scripture, but repugnant to the Word of God."[17]

Roman Catholics—citing Revelation 21:27—do right when they take sin seriously. Wesleyans concur that sin is grave and must be addressed, but believe that the time when God forgives and cleanses our sins is during this life (Matt 6:12; 1 John 1:9). The work of sanctification is a here-and-now preparation for the next life. In the

16. In Crockett, ed., *Four Views on Hell*, 106.
17. Bracher, ed., "Twenty-Five Articles."

same way that we cannot know when Christ will return, we cannot be confident whether our lives will continue or suddenly be taken from us. The follower of Christ should live in a constant state of transparency before the Lord, resting in the ongoing cleansing provided by his blood (1 John 1:7).

Though purgatory passed the three-point theological test we have enumerated, it failed the test of Scripture and may encourage procrastination, discouraging righteousness and constant readiness to meet our maker. For these two reasons, we must turn elsewhere for alternatives to the traditional understanding of Hell.

Universalism

Besides purgatory, another possibility is commonly called "universalism." Arthur Roberts defined the term as the belief that "no person is excluded finally from God's redemption."[18] The renowned early church theologian, Origen of Alexandria (AD 185–254), appeared to have adopted this view, but historically it has been condemned. Recently, there has been mixed reaction to American pastor Rob Bell's book *Love Wins*, parts of which may be interpreted as leaving the door open to universalism.

Sometimes universalism is wrongly equated with "inclusivism," a view advanced by Clark Pinnock. However, Pinnock simply hoped for a "wideness in God's mercy" and emphasized the work of the Holy Spirit through prevenient grace among those who have yet to

18. See "Universalism," in Grider, ed., *Beacon Dictionary of Theology*.

hear a presentation of the gospel.[19] Universalism takes it
to the next level, believing that even those who die shak-
ing their fists at God will eventually be won over by divine
love. The essence of universalism comes through in a few
lines from the poem "Outwitted," by Edwin Markham:

> He drew a circle that shut me out—
> Heretic, rebel, a thing to flout.
> But love and I had the wit to win:
> We drew a circle and took him In!

Will God ultimately draw a circle that takes everyone in? Some Bible passages appear to answer "yes."
Philippians 2:5–11, the familiar *kenosis* passage, speaks
of the time when "every knee should bow" and "every
tongue acknowledge that Jesus Christ is Lord, to the glory
of God the Father" (vv. 10–11). But such an interpretation
neglects the reality that—while God has given everyone
grace to respond to His salvation call, the "light" of John
1:9—some douse that light, refusing to the very end to
avail themselves of the grace freely offered. As C. S. Lewis
observed in *The Great Divorce*, to those who all their lives
refused to say to God, "Thy will be done," to such as these,
God will in the end say: "Thy will be done."[20]

Because 2 Peter 3:9 insists that the Lord does not
wish that any should "perish, but that all should reach
repentance" (RSV), we can pose the question asked by
Rob Bell: *Does God get what God wants*?[21] There is no
indication in this passage that what God wishes somehow
overrides the decision-making ability with which God

19. See Pinnock, *A Wideness in God's Mercy*.
20. Lewis, *The Great Divorce*, 72.
21. Bell, *Love Wins*, 97.

has graced humanity. The short answer to Bell's question is: "No, God does *not* always get what God wants." While 2 Peter 3:9 provides a foundation for the universal *offer* of salvation, it is no guarantee that all will accept that offer. God persuades, but does not coerce.

But let's turn to the three-point test arising from what the Bible says about God's character, the test followed so far when looking at each view of human destiny. How does universalism fare?

1. *Proportionate judgment*—Universalism does not preclude *post mortem* (after death) punishment. The idea that God will one day "empty Hell" implies that Hell in some form exists. Nonetheless, there are other forms of universalism that bypass Hell altogether. A pastor told me of a recent conversation with ministerial colleagues from his denomination. They believe that, no matter how hardened one's heart, God's love will melt away all opposition at the moment of death. So, whether this element in God's character is honored by universalism seems to depend upon the variety of universalism being promoted and whether it allows for any degree of punishment after death.

2. *Love*—While universalism seems big-hearted, one might ask: Towards *whom*? Would it be a loving thing for God to say "your sin doesn't really matter" when God calls us to be holy (1 Pet 1:16)? Returning to my classroom error, was it loving or respectful toward the students who had done their assignment on time when I told the lazy student who had done nothing that an extension was no problem? The parable of the workers in the vineyard (Matt

20:1–16) seems to support God giving "wages" indiscriminately. However, no one in the parable who categorically refused to work received a salary; only those who worked for at least a time were paid. This should be an encouragement to those who come to Christ later in life. They, too, can inherit the kingdom of heaven.[22] But the parable is not meant to give false comfort to those who carelessly sat on the sidelines, to those who all their lives ignored God's call to service, who knew God's standards yet knowingly and consistently flaunted them. It would be decidedly capricious, even *hateful* for God to have two different standards, one for those who "played by the rules" and one for those who tried to circumvent them. Yes, our service to God flows primarily from a loving relationship that begins with our gratitude for salvation, not just for the sake of eventual reward. Nonetheless, hard times for the follower of Christ are bearable in part because we believe—like Jesus encouraged us—that we are storing up "treasures in heaven" (Matt 6:20). On the other hand, if even those who stubbornly refused in this life to serve the master will receive the same wages, does this not undercut one reason for the faithful to persevere? Does it not in some sense make obedience optional?

3. *Holiness*—God is good and just. God's rule in the universe is based upon taking sin seriously. Does universalism—particularly forms that allow no punishment—take sin seriously enough? When an individual has had countless opportunities to respond to the salvation offer, yet obstinately refuses to do so,

22. Bruce, *Hard Sayings of Jesus*, 197–98.

inflicting damage and hurt on others along the way, can God in the end just say: "Never mind"? Some oppose the death penalty as administered by human courts in part because of confidence that God will one day judge fairly. Universalism may undercut our willingness to leave the "hard cases" in God's hands, cases like Timothy McVeigh, the Oklahoma City bomber.

The five maidens of Matthew 25 were unprepared for the bridegroom's return. Coming back from buying more oil, they found the door shut. As followers of Christ filled with God's love, we hope that a door once shut conceivably could be opened again, but the parable makes no such promise. Surely wisdom demands erring on the side of caution. Our view of last things should not encourage others to hope for second chances that God has never guaranteed, to "sin, that grace may abound" (Rom 6:1). We should not presume that God will veto the free choices of rebels, forcibly corralling the prodigal sons and daughters who repeatedly refused in this life to make their way back home.

Conclusion

Are there second chances after death? Purgatory offers hope of a second chance for many (not all), while universalism pictures a God who refuses to exclude anyone, overwhelmingly drawing all into the kingdom of Heaven. Between the two possibilities, purgatory better responds to the three-fold theological test of proportionality, love, and holiness. However, both purgatory and universalism fail to measure up to the teaching of Scripture. Holy living ideally arises out of our love for God and our desire to please him. While we might wish that all would operate primarily from such a positive motivation, many have not yet moved to that level of relationship. In the meantime, are we willing to eliminate a more shallow but valid motivation for holy living in the here-and-now?

Where does that leave us? Is there no alternative that is at once true to the Bible and true to the character of God? The short answer is "yes." But before examining that view in detail, let us turn in the next chapter to some philosophical assumptions about the nature of human existence that—in any discussion of Hell—are always lurking just beneath the surface.

For Discussion

1. Discuss the author's story of the students who turned in papers on time and the late student who received an extension. How would you have felt if you were the on-time students? The late student? Do you agree with the author's suggestion that God blindly pardoning evildoers is a form of disrespect or hatred toward those who during this life lived a righteous life?

2. The author admitted that purgatory passed the three-fold test of proportionate judgment, love and holiness, yet in the end rejected purgatory. On what grounds was this rejection made? Debate whether purgatory is a viable alternative to the vision of Hell as unending, conscious torment.

3. Is avoiding future punishment a sufficient motivation for living a holy life now? What positive motivation should we also have?

4. One important tenet in Wesleyan theology is what is commonly called "free will" (enabled by God's grace). In your judgment, does universalism honor the free will of the individual? Discuss this especially in relation to the C. S. Lewis quote cited by the author.

5

What *Are* We, Anyways?

Your candle burned out long before your legend ever did.
—SIR ELTON JOHN

Thomas "Stonewall" Jackson was a legendary Confederate general during the American Civil War. Mortally wounded by friendly fire during the battle of Chancellorsville on May 2, 1863, history recorded his final words: "Let us cross over the river, and rest under the shade of the trees." Jackson's vision recalls Greek mythology where death is pictured as a journey across the river Styx, the divide between the earth and the underworld, with Phlegyas as the boatman who ferries passengers to the other side.

What happens at the moment of death? Is it like Stonewall Jackson and the Greek legends say, a journey across a river to a peaceful and radiant destination? For some, will that crossing lead to a place of punishment? On the other hand, is death simply a version of the old saying, "Turn out the lights, the party's over"? Is it Elton John's "candle in the wind," burned out, extinguished? Is death existence surrendering to non-existence, a quick descent into nothingness? For those who have read the first four chapters of this book, this may seem like a fruitless detour. Yet some consideration of this question is necessary to make sense of conditional immortality, an alternative view of destiny that will be presented in later chapters.

The answer to the question of what lies immediately beyond the moment we breathe our last will depend in part upon our answer to another question philosophical in nature: *What is a human being?* Christian theologians have responded in two ways:

1. *dualism*—Many have followed the dualistic lead of ancient Greek philosophy, which views the person as made up of two separate components, namely, "spirit" (soul) and "matter" (body). In this conception, the body is the prison house of the soul, a temporary and corrupt vessel from which an immortal and pure soul must make its escape.

2. *holism*—Others, following in the footsteps of Old Testament thought, teach "holism" (or monism), that there exists a fundamental unity in the human person between flesh and the breath of life (Hebrew *nephesh*) that God breathes into us, just as he breathed into Adam (Gen 2:7). For the holist, the "soul" is not like a ghost that could live a disembodied life, hanging around cemeteries or haunting houses. Rather, it is the animating principle that will cease to operate at the moment of death.

Dualism and holism creep into our language in subtle ways. "We found her remains in the river," the coroner reports to distraught parents. Does this not imply that some essential part of the person has departed? On the other hand, a little girl might complain: "Mommy, I hurt." What does she mean? She is trying to say that her *arm* hurts, but she has made no distinction between her bodily member and who she is. For all practical purposes, they are one and the same.

This is the question of theological anthropology, the study of what makes up the human being. Besides the evidence of Scripture, anthropology is a key piece in putting together the puzzle of human destiny. If you are a dualist, then you believe that death is never complete. Only a part of us dies, namely, our body. The other part of us, our immortal soul, will at the expiration of our body leave its mortal house, like a hand withdrawn from a glove. The old gospel hymn captured this sentiment:

> *I'll fly away, O glory! I'll fly away.*
> *When I die, Hallelujah! By and by*
> *I'll fly away.*

The New Testament contains passages that suggest a dualistic interpretation. On the cross, Jesus told the repentant thief: "I tell you the truth, today you will be with me in paradise" (Luke 23:43), implying that Jesus expected to exist elsewhere immediately at death.[1] When we turn to Paul's writings, we may ask the question: How far from Plato's concept of the body as a prison is Paul's metaphor of our earthly existence being like a "tent" (2 Cor 5:1)? In verses 8–9 of the same chapter, the apostle

---

1. But some early Greek manuscripts read: "I tell you the truth today, you will be with me in paradise." See Ellis, *Gospel of Luke*, 268–69.

spoke of being either "at home in the body" or "at home with the Lord." Paul's "visions and revelations" included being "caught up to the third heaven." What was the nature of that journey? Paul himself was unsure: "Whether it was in the body or out of the body I do not know—God knows" (2 Cor 12:2).

Yet other biblical evidence—some would argue the preponderance—points in a holistic direction. When Herod sent soldiers to kill the children two years and younger living in Bethlehem, Matthew discerned a fulfillment of Jeremiah's prophecy: "A voice is heard in Ramah, weeping and great mourning, Rachel weeping for her children and refusing to be comforted, because *they are no more*" (Matt 2:18, italics added). Job 14:1–2 shares the pessimism of the weeping Rachel: "A mortal, born of woman, few of days and full of trouble, comes up like a flower and withers, flees like a shadow and does not last." For the holist/monist, to die is to cease to exist.

Ezekiel 37 provides the clearest Old Testament picture of the holistic worldview. The Spirit of the LORD led the prophet to the edge of a valley full of bones. He asked: "Son of man, can these bones live?" Ezekiel replied: "O Sovereign LORD, you alone know" (v. 3). God commanded his prophet to prophesy, and as he did, the bones begin to rattle, coming together with tendons and flesh to form bodies. But the bodies were not alive—why not? They still had no breath. Again, God commanded Ezekiel to prophesy, to call the four winds to breathe life into the slain (v. 9). When the prophet did so, "they came to life and stood up on their feet—a vast army" (v. 10). In Ezekiel's vision, the human being was not an immortal soul residing in a body. Rather, it was a body animated by the breath of life given and withdrawn at God's pleasure.

Daniel 12:1–4 goes one step further. In his vision of the last day, the righteous will not be raised only for a time, but to "everlasting life" (v. 2). Others will be raised to "shame and everlasting contempt." This may be seen as a bridge to the more explicit New Testament teaching on resurrection.

Paul, a Christian with Jewish roots, propagated a modified version of holism. The same individual who had speculated about his mystical vision of heaven in 2 Corinthians 12 is more down to earth in 1 Corinthians 15. Paul began by speaking of the "gospel I preached to you," the firm ground on which "you have taken your stand" (v. 1). And what were the key elements of this gospel?

1. Jesus died;

2. Jesus was buried;

3. God raised Jesus to life on the third day.

Paul employed the term "asleep" as a synonym of "the dead" (v. 20). The apostle was not dualistically describing bodies apart from "immortal souls," a term never used in the chapter. Rather, he was speaking in holistic terms, of the "dead" who are "raised" (v. 35). His whole argument throughout the chapter was that what is "perishable" will be "raised imperishable" (v. 42). What is "mortal" must be clothed with "immortality" (v. 54).

For his part, John Wesley was clearly a dualist. In his treatise on *Original Sin* (1757), he taught that the natural image of God in the human person includes an immortal soul.[2] However, Wesley overlooked the context of the passage in question (Gen 1:26), that after expelling Adam and Eve from the garden, the LORD put an angel on guard at the tree of life expressly to *prevent* humanity from eating of the tree, and living forever (Gen 3:22).

In our day, Christians have slipped into a strange mishmash of language regarding the hereafter. Though dualism is our default, we still want to use bodily language to talk about our loved ones and their new abode. So, when a young boy with multiple sclerosis dies, you'll hear family members at the funeral say: "Thank God, our son has a new body now." Yet how can this be? Even dualists have traditionally anticipated the reunion of the resurrected body and immortal soul, but when does this happen? Both Jesus and Paul speak of resurrection as happening only at the return of Christ (John 5:28–29; 1 Thess 4:13–18).

Even if dualism is accepted, one must ask: *How can a disembodied spirit currently have a new body, when Jesus has not yet returned and the resurrection has not yet occurred?* As much as we might wish our Uncle Harry is playing golf in heaven, or our deceased grandma is busy baking her favorite cookies, these are all *bodily* activities. How can they be performed by spirits? No wonder critics think Christians are confused!

As the early Christians faced death under various Roman emperors, it was not immortality of the soul that gave them comfort. Rather, it was the strong belief that because Jesus rose, they too would one day rise. Dead bodies—whether still whole or long disintegrated into

2. See Collins, *Theology of John Wesley*, 52.

their constituent molecules—will be recreated by God and given back the breath of life. They will live again! And God, the source of that breath of life, has promised never again to withdraw it from the righteous. 1 Thessalonians 4:18 ends with this exhortation: "So comfort and encourage each other with these words." And what were those words? It was the promise of the resurrection, that at the return of Christ, "all Christians who have died will rise from their graves" (4:16, NLT). This is new creation (Rev 21:5), God bringing the non-existent back into glorious and permanent being, making them over again, new and improved, death being swallowed up in victory (1 Cor 15:54). What a promise!

The holistic view of the human person explains why the Apostles' Creed made no mention of the soul's immortality, but instead affirmed new creation: "I believe in the resurrection of the body . . . and the life everlasting." The life is "everlasting" because we will share the immortality gifted to us by God. To date, only God is immortal (1 Tim 6:16), but a change in the order of things will one day be complete, since Christ "has destroyed death and has brought life and immortality to light through the gospel" (2 Tim 1:10). The life without end denied us in the Garden of Eden will one day be the inheritance of all the righteous. We'll get to sink our teeth into that delicious fruit after all.

So Where Is My Loved One Now?

As we have seen, Christians differ in their understanding of the make-up of a human being. Some are dualists, and others are holists. Dualists see in certain New Testament references an "intermediate state" where the righteous are at peace with Jesus and the wicked suffer, awaiting final judgment (Luke 16:19–31; 23:43). On the other hand, holists take the metaphor of "sleep" (John 11:11; 1 Thess 4:15, KJV) as indicating non-existence pending God's new creation at the resurrection (Rev 22:1–2). Given this polarization, how shall we answer the grieving relative who asks us: "Where is my loved one now?"

Our disagreements as believers should not obscure where we do agree. With the early Christians, we affirm: "I believe in the resurrection." Likewise, when Jesus expired on the cross, he prayed: "Father, I entrust my spirit into your hands!" (Luke 23:46, NLT). So we can say confidently to the grieving: *"They are in God's hands, awaiting the resurrection."*

Conclusion

Having seen the biblical and philosophical underpinnings of holism, in the next chapter we will lay out the details of conditional immortality, a neglected view of human destiny. We will discover that—while not perfect—conditional immortality does the best job of any view explaining relevant Bible passages, staying true to God's nature of loving holiness and the divine practice of equitable justice.

For Discussion

1. One criticism of holism is that it reduces the human being to the level of animals. After all, if we have no immortal soul, then what makes us different from a cat or a chimpanzee? From a holistic frame of reference and citing the Bible, how would you answer this critique?

2. When comforting those who are mourning, which viewpoint do you find more soothing, holism or dualism? Why? Are you satisfied with the answer the author gave to the question, "Where is my loved one now?" Why or why not?

6

The Bright Side of Destiny

Resurrection, Reward, and Immortality

I am making everything new!

—JESUS (REV 21:5)

L arry King, the retired talk show host, shocked his
guests when he revealed his posthumous wish. "I
want to be frozen," he said, "on the hope that they'll find
whatever I died of and they'll bring me back." When asked
why he would want to do that, his answer was telling.
He admitted that his "biggest fear" was death, because
"I don't think I'm going anywhere." Instead, he agreed
wholeheartedly that he wanted to "live forever."[1]

What King admitted in a moment of candor is the
secret wish of most human beings. We do not so much
crave *any* type of existence beyond the grave as we desire
continued *bodily* existence. For all the aches and pains,
sicknesses and disappointments that this life brings, it

1. Lewis, "Larry King Shocks Guests."

45

also gives us incredible benefits. In the flesh we know the happiness of a delicious meal, the beauty of a scintillating sunset, or the thrill of the wind catching our hair as we ski down a mountain pass. Because we have bodies, we are comforted by the reassuring hug of a friend and excited by the sensual touch of a lover. These are good gifts from God, so it's not surprising that we don't want to lose those gifts.

Preparing for a sermon on the next life, I posted a question on a social network, hoping for responses: "What happens when we die?" Brian (not his real name), an avowed agnostic, quickly replied: "We decompose." And Brian is partly right, but is that the whole story? Do we simply become worm food, recycled back into Mother Nature's molecular stew, ready for her to brew up some new life form from what used to be us? Will we never again know conscious existence?

Jesus and Lazarus (John 11:1–44)

One of the clearest Bible passages supporting a holistic worldview as it relates to the believer's destiny is the story of Lazarus. He had already been dead four days, rotting in a smelly tomb. Jesus had purposely delayed his coming so that there could be no question about the particulars of the case. Lazarus wasn't just "mostly dead," as Miracle Max of the movie *Princess Bride* announced regarding his rigid young patient. Lazarus was just plain dead. The Lord had taken his time, but to what end? It was so that his disciples might believe (v. 15). Martha, the sister of the dead man, embodied the prevailing Jewish belief at the time regarding the next life. When Jesus reassured her that her brother "will rise again" (v. 23), Martha answered with the standard response of the faithful Jew: "I know he will rise again in the last day" (v. 24). God had already revealed this through the writings of the prophet Daniel (see Dan 12:1–4). But now Jesus takes it a step further. He replies in v. 25: "I am the resurrection and the life. He who believes in me will live, even though he dies; and whoever lives and believes in me will never die. Do you believe this?"

The verse works something like my bifocals. Part of the lens—the upper portion—is helpful for seeing objects at a distance, like road signs when I'm driving my car. The lower part is meant for viewing things that are close up, such as a book or a computer screen. Lazarus is the "close up" part of the lens, the resurrection that Jesus will perform in just a few minutes. But the "far away" aspect applies to all believers, the resurrection that will happen at the end of time when the Son of Man comes to judge (see John 5:28–29).

What exactly is Jesus saying in John 11:25? Let's take the verse apart, phrase by phrase:

"I am the resurrection and the life." By claiming a power that Martha and the others present knew only belonged to God, Jesus is making a bold claim to deity. This is the "close-up" part of the bivocals. It was primarily a present claim made by Jesus standing in front of the tomb that day, but also one with future ramifications.

"He who believes in me will live, even though he dies." Here we are looking through *both* parts of the bifocals. Jesus is referring to an event close-up in time, to Lazarus the believer, now dead and buried but whom Jesus would

soon raise to life before their very eyes. Yet there is a further horizon, the last day when Christ would return to judge all (Matt 25:31–46). This is the general resurrection, when all humanity must stand before his judgment seat, the place where the believer—justified by grace through faith—will be rewarded according to his or her deeds, the irrefutable evidence of God's saving and transforming work (Eph 2:8–10; 2 Cor 5:10).

"And whoever lives and believes in me will never die." Our eyes are now focused only on the distant horizon. How so? The phrase "will never die" clearly could not be applied to Lazarus, since he eventually would expire again, despite Jesus having raised him from the stinking tomb. Instead, Jesus is looking to the end of time when the trumpet will sound, when what is "mortal" must be clothed with "immortality" (1 Cor 15:51, 53–54). At the last day, God will grant resurrected believers the gift of immortality (2 Tim 1:10; Rom 6:23b; Gal 6:8b), a gift conditioned upon how we responded to God's offer during this life as symbolized by the "book of life" (Rev 20:12). Paul affirms: "And if the Spirit of him who raised Jesus from the dead is living in you, he who raised Christ from the dead will also give life to your mortal bodies through his Spirit, who lives in you" (Rom 8:11). What a promise!

The Bright Side of Destiny:
Living Forever in the New Creation

What will life post-resurrection be like for the believer? We wish the Bible provided the clarity of a high-resolution digital camera. Instead, we might be forgiven for thinking we're looking at an impressionist painting by one of the French masters! To change the metaphor, the Bible only lets us see the tip of the iceberg. Underneath the water, invisible to us, is the remainder of the reality of the new creation.

What we do know is that Jesus will make "everything new" (Rev 21:5). Realizing that the symbolism of Revelation can be pushed too far, we can still make preliminary observations about the nature of resurrected life in the kingdom of God:

1. *The descent of the "New Jerusalem."* While Paul pictures Christ's return as those living and those resurrected being "caught up" to meet the Lord in the air (1 Thess 4:17), John's vision is of the New Jerusalem "coming down out of heaven from God, prepared as a bride beautifully dressed for her husband" (Rev 21:2). We can only imagine the beauty of this city, the "Father's house" with many "dwellings" (John 14:1–3). It is here that Jesus will transport his followers when he returns: "And if I go and prepare a place for you, I will come back and take you to be with me that you may also be where I am" (v. 3).[2]

2. *Our lives will overflow with worship to God.* The revelation that Jesus gave to John on Patmos is clear. Like the twenty-four elders and the four living creatures (Rev 4:6–13; 19:4–5), we will join in worship to the Lamb seated upon the throne.

3. *We will be part of joyous community.* It is striking that what we do in the new creation will be done to-

---

2. See Carson, *Gospel according to John*, 488, where this passage is interpreted as happening at Christ's return.

gether. Here on earth, part of life in the community of faith, the church, is eating together. Good food will be an important part of existence, as symbolized by the "wedding supper of the Lamb" (19:9) and a "tree of life" on each side of the river of life, each bearing "twelve crops of fruit" (22:2). Kenneth Grider suggested that we may undertake projects together, an activity hinted at by the parable of the ten minas (Luke 19:11–27).[3] Though there will be no marriage as we know it on earth (Matt 22:22–33), we will experience laughter and joyful relationships as transformed, resurrected persons.

4. *Our focus will be on the joys of the present, with no fear of the future.* Revelation 7:17b affirms that God will "wipe away every tear from their eyes." The Lord will cheer our hearts and abolish sadness. We will live in joyous service, the kingdom of God as our inheritance (Matt 25:34; Rev 5:10).

Conclusion

Because the resurrection is for the disciple of Jesus the gateway to life unending, Easter becomes the highest Christian celebration on the church calendar. Rob Staples affirmed: "Christ is not the *only* one to be raised; He is the *first* one."[4] Jesus has conquered death, and so shall we! N. T. Wright chided the church for placing her accent upon Christmas while downplaying Easter: "Take Christmas away, and in biblical terms you lose two chap-

---

3. Grider, *Wesleyan-Holiness Theology*, 547.
4. Rob Staples, in Dunning, ed., *Second Coming*, 258.

ters at the front of Matthew and Luke, nothing else. Take Easter away, and you don't have a New Testament. . . . This is our greatest day. We should put the flags out."[5] He suggests an eight day festival of celebration, beginning on Easter Sunday. Wright is surely correct that one day is not enough, especially after the somber forty day Lenten season.

While the New Testament leaves room for debate between dualists and holists, there is no question about the central event of salvation history. The resurrection is the "bright side of destiny." It is here that we as Christians stake our claim; it is here that we hang all of our hopes (1 Cor 15:17). Because Jesus lives in bodily form, we, too, shall have a new, enduring body. Christ is risen! He is risen indeed.

For Discussion

1. The old spiritual wishes us a good outcome: "In that great, getting' up mornin', fare thee well, fare thee well." According to the holistic vision, what is the sequence of events for the believer upon his or her death?

2. Some have described the period between death and resurrection as "soul sleep." The English word "cemetery" comes from the Greek *koimeterion*, meaning "sleeping place" or "dormitory."[6] What sense of the passage of time does a sleeping person have? For the believer, is the image of sleeping a comforting one?

5. Wright, *Surprised by Hope*, 256–57.
6. See Harper, "Cemetery."

3. The holistic worldview teaches that an individual ceases to exist at death, pending the resurrection. From a biblical standpoint, how might a holist account for "ghosts"?

7

The Dark Side of Destiny

Resurrection, Punishment, and Destruction

> The eyes of the LORD are everywhere,
> keeping watch on the wicked and the good.
> —PROV 15:3

In the previous chapter, we examined the resurrection with its rewards for the righteous. The most important reward was that of immortality, the opportunity to live forever in peaceful community, worshipfully engaging in meaningful tasks, celebrating the presence of God. That is the bright side of destiny.

But sadly, since there is a dark side to history, there must also be a dark side to destiny. The centuries offer numerous examples of tyrants, ruthless men and women. Like drunken drivers, they leave in their wake misery, suffering, and death. As ardently as we might wish God to settle all accounts in this life, too often the wicked get away with their crimes, thumbing their nose at any higher authority, unrepentant for their sins, outside the reach of human justice.

Yet Proverbs 15:3 affirms that God is fully aware of injustice. Indeed, the "servant of the Lord" pictured by Isaiah—a figure interpreted by Christians as the Messiah—is keenly concerned that justice prevail:

> Here is my servant, whom I uphold, my chosen one in whom I delight. I will put my Spirit on him and he will bring justice to the nations. He will not shout or cry out, or raise his voice in the streets. A bruised reed he will not break, and a smoldering wick he will not snuff out. In faithfulness he will bring forth justice; he will not falter or be discouraged till he establishes justice on earth. In his law the people of the islands will put their hope. (Isa 42:1–4)

We saw in earlier chapters what "justice" looks like from the divine perspective. It conforms to the *lex talionis*, the law of retaliation requiring a measured response, the punishment fitting the crime. Secondly, it reflects the character of God, which is love (1 John 4:8). Finally, it takes into account the holiness of God, a God who—because of his holy nature—cannot brush off sin as inconsequential. The writer to the Hebrews captured this in a word picture, warning: "Our God is a consuming fire" (Heb 12:29). It is this three-fold test of fairness, love, and holiness, that any view of punishment and Hell must pass. Further, we have to ask: *Does it agree with the general message of Scripture?* Any interpretation must make sense not only of a given passage, but must square with the broad sweep of what the Bible teaches.

In this chapter, we will present the evidence for a minority view of Hell. In the past, it has been called annihilationism, but more recently "conditional immortality." By the end of the chapter, the reader will see that it alone best responds to the criteria laid out above.

What Is "Conditional Immortality"?

Conditional immortality is the conviction that both final life for believers and final death for the wicked are contingent upon how one responds here on earth to God's offer of life. Paul affirmed before the philosophers in Athens that only in God do we "live and move and have our being" (Acts 17:28). This is true not only for our earthly existence, but our ultimate destiny. God has placed before us both life and death. Immortality—what Paul calls "inheriting the kingdom of God"—is conditioned upon the holiness that is only acquired when we voluntarily open our lives to the transforming divine presence (1 Cor 6:9–11). Shutting ourselves off from God's presence in this life is to shut ourselves off from the source of being in the life to come.

As we have seen, immortality belongs only to God (1 Tim 6:16), but one thing is clear: It is only to the righteous that God will grant immortality after the resurrection. Because our first parents rebelled against God by eating of the tree of the knowledge of good and evil, God took the precaution of posting an angel to guard the tree of life (Gen 3:24). What was God's fear? If humans ate of the tree of life, they would "live forever" (3:22). Importantly, trees of life appear again in Revelation 22:2, where they blossom on both sides of the river of life, giving fruit every month. Unlike in Eden, no longer is access denied; citizens of the New Jerusalem will freely partake of the fruit, a symbol of the immortality that God has now bestowed upon them. In the meantime, we live out our earthly existence as mere mortals, a "mist that appears for a little while and then vanishes" (Jas 4:14).

Hell: Non-Being as Ultimate Punishment

The New Testament is not explicit about the punishment of the wicked. Paul does affirm that both "trouble and distress" and "wrath and anger" await "those who are self-seeking and who reject the truth," those who "follow evil" (Rom 2:8–9). But post-resurrection at the judgment seat (Rev 20:11–15), how will God differentiate—for example—between mass murderers and those who simply stubbornly refused God's offer of eternal life? A clue may be found in Luke 12:42–48. There, Jesus recounted the parable of the wise manager, a parable about his second coming and the judgment that follows. The servant who knows his master will return yet does not prepare himself will be "beaten with many blows" (v. 47). However, the one who is not aware that his master will return yet who "does things deserving of punishment will be beaten with few blows" (v. 48). Admittedly, this parable does not answer all questions. Nevertheless, it does establish that God is able to judge individuals on a case-by-case basis and assign appropriate punishment depending upon the circumstances, which may include whether an individual ever received a clear gospel presentation.

Elsewhere, Jesus warns us repeatedly about the reality of Hell. Obviously, he was concerned that we get the message! But we must ask: *What is the nature of that Hell?* Is it unending, conscious torment as we have been taught to believe? The biblical evidence points in another direction. N. T. Wright noted that the most common word Jesus used to refer to Hell is the Greek term *Gehenna*. This was "the rubbish heap outside the southwest corner of the old city of Jerusalem."[1] The image is of refuse being burned up, incinerated and reduced to ashes. It is the "unquenchable fire" to which John the Baptist referred in his preaching, a flame that burns up the chaff (Matt 3:12). This is the plain meaning of Jesus' warning in Matthew 10:28, where he admonishes his listeners to fear God, the one who can "destroy both soul and body in hell" (Matt 10:28). Here, the image is not only the destruction of the body but of the very life principle that animates it. Paul writes: "For the wages of sin is death, but the gift of God is eternal life in Jesus Christ our Lord" (Rom 6:23). In this verse, "death" is the "wages of sin." One who is dead no longer exists. It is the opposite destiny from those who receive God's free gift of eternal life.

Likewise, non-existence is the most natural meaning of the term "perish" in John's gospel. What is arguably the most famous verse in the New Testament—John 3:16—is so familiar that we may overlook its simplicity. There are only two options: Either we "believe," resulting in eternal life, or else we "perish." The same binary scenario plays out in John 10:28, where Jesus the shepherd gives "eternal life" to his sheep. Because of his gift, "they shall never per-

1. Wright, *Surprised by Hope*, 175.

ish." God's desire—which sadly will be thwarted by those most stubborn—is that no one "perish," but that everyone should "come to repentance" (2 Pet 3:9). Often overlooked is the immediate context of this verse. Peter says that because of God's word, the heavens and the earth were brought into existence (3:5). In the same way, by a word from God's mouth, "the present heavens and earth have been stored up for fire. They are being kept for the day of judgment, when ungodly people will be destroyed" (3:7, NLT). So in this passage, the concepts of existence, destruction, and perishing appear close together. The lesson is sobering: To be destroyed by God is to perish, to pass into non-being. It is the "second death" as symbolized by the lake of fire into which all those whose names are not found in the book of life are thrown (Rev 20:15). Truly, our God is a "consuming fire" (Heb 12:29).

Elsewhere, Paul employs the same eternal life vs. destruction terminology. In Galatians 6:7–8, he warns of the ultimate outcome of sinful living, comparing it to seed time and harvest. "Do not be deceived," he cautioned. "God cannot be mocked. A man reaps what he sows." Paul allows for only two outcomes: "The one who sows to please his sinful nature, from that nature will reap destruction; the one who sows to please the Spirit, from the spirit will reap eternal life." Summarizing the biblical evidence, Clark Pinnock concluded: "The Bible uses the language of death and destruction, of ruin and perishing, when it speaks of the fate of the impenitent wicked. It uses the imagery of fire that consumes whatever is thrown into it; linking together the images of fire and destruction suggests annihilation."[2] This is in line with Arnobius (died

2. In Crockett, ed., *Four Views on Hell*, 144.

AD 330), an early Christian thinker who argued against Plato's concept of the immortal soul, calling such an idea "gross hubris." As for the wicked, they will be "consumed in a long protracted torment with raging fire."[3] Here, the key word is "consumed," a cessation of being preceded by punishment that the wicked have merited.

Conditional Immortality: A Balanced Approach

Many of the objections to Hell coalesce around the grotesque image of God torturing human beings indefinitely. The vision of Hell as unending, conscious torment pictures God as a sadist. God's moral image in us—severely damaged, though never fully lost—makes even the nonbeliever recoil before such a specter. The traditional view of Hell might square with God's holiness, but it denies God's love and obliterates any sense of proportionality in punishment.

Conditional immortality, on the other hand, is a balanced approach, honoring both God's character of loving holiness and human free will enabled by God's grace. As such, conditional immortality vindicates God's justice, placing moral responsibility back upon the individual where it belongs. Eternal existence belongs only to God and to those to whom he shall choose to grant it in the future. It is God's good gift, and not an inherent characteristic of our human nature. As something offered by God, immortality comes with conditions, primarily a willingness to give up our sin and submit our lives to God. When we as individuals stubbornly refuse to meet

3. Cited by Fudge, *Fire that Consumes*, 291.

those requirements then add evil offenses on top of them, what should we expect? God will then be justified in meting out to the wicked measured punishment in a "lake of fire" (Rev 20:14) before they are consumed, slipping back into nothingness, the permanent non-being that is the only possible condition of persons permanently separated from the life of God.

For Discussion

1. What is your reaction to the concept of "conditional immortality"? In recent years, there has been what Edward Fudge calls an "evangelical recovery" of the minority view, including prominent scholars such as John R. W. Stott and I. Howard Marshall.[4] Why do you think the church across the ages—apart from Arnobius—has been reluctant to embrace this idea?

2. Of the various views presented in this book—unending, conscious torment, purgatory, universalism, and conditional immortality—which to your mind is the most convincing? Why?

3. In your view, does the author make his case for proportionate punishment preceding annihilation of the wicked? Are there other Bible passages that you would cite to support or critique this idea? Is there another version of the "dark side of destiny" not addressed in this book that you prefer?

4. Ibid., 349–50.

8

Answering Objections

The conditional immortality (annihilationist) position has its detractors. Apart from those who critique it for lacking advocates historically, others are reluctant to abandon the traditional view of Hell since only it appears to adequately explain a few key Bible passages. Two such Scripture verses are Matthew 25:46 and Mark 9:48.

Matthew 25:46—Eternal Punishment, Eternal Life

The parable of the sheep and the goats takes place at the time of final judgment, when "the Son of Man comes in his glory, and all the angels with him" (25:31). The "cursed" are those who neglected "the least of these" (v. 45), while the "righteous" are those who fed the stranger, gave him something to drink, clothed the naked and visited those who were sick or in prison (vv. 34–36). The Lord will punish the cursed with "eternal punishment," but reward the righteous with "eternal life." In both instances, the Greek word for "eternal" is *aiōnios*. The argument can be made that if the punishment is finite, then so is the life inherited by the righteous.

Yet must *aiōnios* always be understood as unending in duration? Jude 7 speaks of Sodom being destroyed by "eternal fire." Yet there, the "fire" clearly is not everlasting, i.e. constant in duration. Rather, as Edward Fudge noted, it is the *results* of the fire that will last forever.[1] "Everlasting" can therefore also mean irreversible or final. With this in mind, Clark Pinnock commented on the meaning of Matthew 25:46:

> I admit that the interpretation of hell as everlasting conscious torment can be found in this verse if one wishes to, especially if the adjective "conscious" is smuggled into the phrase "eternal punishment" (as is common). But there are considerations that line up the meaning with the larger body of evidence. In this text, Jesus does not define the nature either of eternal life or eternal death. He says there will be two destinies and leaves it there. This perspective gives us the freedom to interpret the saying about hell either as everlasting conscious torment (eternal punishing) or as irreversible destruction (eternal punishment). The text allows for both interpretations because it only teaches the finality of the judgment, not its precise nature.[2]

We see this meaning in popular English usage. The host of the television program "Millionaire" often asks the contestant: "Is that your *final* answer?" Once the contestant says "yes," there is no chance to reverse it. Likewise, when Jesus has pronounced his verdict on the sheep and

1. Ibid., 137.
2. In Crockett, ed., *Four Views on Hell*, 156.

the goats, it will have eternal (irreversible) consequences, with either life or death as the final outcome. This concurs with Paul's teaching in 2 Thessalonians 1:8–10, where the disobedient are "shut out from the presence of the Lord" and suffer "everlasting destruction," a phrase most naturally interpreted as their final and utter ruin. Cut off from the "majesty of (the Lord's) power" (v. 9), they ultimately will perish.

Some object that "irreversible death" is no punishment at all. However, as has been noted above, annihilation does not rule out proportional punishment preceding it. Further, while final destruction does not rise to the level that unending, conscious torment does, it surely is a severe form of retribution, death being the greatest punishment that a governing authority can inflict upon a person. A stronger objection would be that conditional immortality fails the test of love, if love is remedial, always seeks the redemption of the person in question. How is annihilation in any way redemptive or corrective? The only answer possible is that for any individual who during this life persistently and stubbornly refuses correction or redemption, God in the end will accede to their wish for non-being. Surely this is more loving and proportionate than inflicting everlasting torture upon such an individual.

Mark 9:48—"Their Worm Does Not Die, and the Fire Is Not Quenched"

Jesus cited this saying from Isaiah 66:24 in the context of individuals who are the cause of "little ones" sinning. It is far better to lose a hand or an eye than to be "thrown into hell" (9:46; Gk. *Gehenna*). The Lord goes on to explain the nature of Hell as a place where "their worm does not die, and the fire is not quenched." Some have seen in this quotation a reference to unending, conscious torment, but is this what Isaiah meant, or what Jesus was teaching? It is more likely that the Lord is saying that losing one of our bodily members is better than our entire body being destroyed.

The picture from Isaiah 66:24 is of those who have rebelled against God. "All mankind" on that day will look upon the "dead bodies" of the rebels. Edward Fudge described the scene and its significance: "The worms and the fire both signify a total destruction, and both make this a 'loathsome' scene. It is not a picture of pain but of shame; the righteous who view it react with disgust not with pity. The sight and smell of burning, maggot-ridden corpses is loathsome, contemptible, abhorrent, repugnant, and repulsive."[3] It is clear in his vision that Isaiah sees the worms not as instruments of endless torture but as a means of bringing decay to that from which the breath of life has departed.

Hell and the Missionary Impulse

A final objection that is sometimes raised against the conditional immortality view of human destiny is connected with the missionary enterprise. If we don't believe that the wicked will suffer for all eternity in Hell, will this not lessen the urgency of preaching? Undoubtedly this could

3. Fudge, *Fire that Consumes*, 77.

be the case for some, but it need not be the consequence of adopting an annihilationist position. Jesus recognized that the "thief" comes "only to steal and kill and destroy." However, Jesus announced: "I have come that they may have life, and have it to the full" (John 10:10). In the same spirit, the missionary goes out to spread the Good News of salvation, that destruction need not be our destiny. Instead, God ardently desires for us to inherit eternal life through Jesus Christ. That positive and hopeful message is fuel more than adequate to keep the "engine" of missions running at full speed.

Conclusion

The conditional immortality viewpoint—though a minor stance throughout history—is gaining ground in our time. It rings true to the whole witness of Scripture, respecting the theological concern of divine proportion in judgment and simultaneously honoring the loving and holy character of God. Though objections may be lodged against it, these are being answered, leading thinking Christians to take a new look at a long neglected option.

For Discussion

1. What meaning may the Greek term *aiōnios* carry? Is the concept of "irreversible punishment" as satisfying to your mind as "punishment without end"? Why or why not?

2. If you were to make a list of the five top reasons we send missionaries, what would be on your list?

Do you agree that the motivation for missions would be unaffected if tomorrow the vast majority of Christians adopted the conditional immortality viewpoint?

Epilogue

Generations have loved the story of the *Velveteen Rabbit*. Worn ragged over many years by the affection of the Boy, Rabbit's skin is threadbare, the satin of his ears faded, his body stained with dirt. When the Boy contracts scarlet fever, Rabbit stays at his side, seeing him through to health again. Later, the doctor orders that all germ-infested bed linens be burned. The maid throws them all into a bag for the dump, and mercilessly tosses Rabbit inside. But before the gardener can build a fire, a fairy appears. For Rabbit's faithful service to his owner, in an instant of magic, the fairy transforms the stuffed toy into a *real* Rabbit.

Many see in this children's tale an allegory of Christian faith. At the end of the story, the Velveteen Rabbit is spared destruction by fire; instead, he is transported to a level of existence that he had never known. Likewise, for the faithful Christian, the story ends with transformation from mortality to immortality, from what is comparatively unreal to what is *real*. God's gift to us will be life without end, communion with God and other believers that far surpasses anything previously experienced.

The Good News is that God has a gift for those who will receive it. Paul writes in Romans 6:23: "For the wages of sin is death, but the gift of God is eternal life in Jesus Christ our Lord." John 3:16 is more than a poster people hold up at football games. In that classic passage, the choices are clear: we can "perish" or we can receive "everlasting life." Immortality is not something we innately possess. Rather, it is Jesus himself who has "destroyed death and has brought life and immortality to light through the gospel" (2 Tim 1:10).

Hell to Avoid

There is a dark side to destiny. Jesus repeatedly warned of Hell (Gk. *Gehenna*), comparing it to the city dump where trashed was burned up (Mark 9:47–49). The Lord is evoking Isaiah 66:24. Edward Fudge commented on the passage: "This worm devours, and what it eats, in Isaiah's picture that Jesus quotes here without amendment, is already dead. Assisting the consuming worm in this disintegration is a consuming, irresistible fire."[1] John in his vision of the final judgment calls this fiery end for the wicked the "second death" (Rev 20:14). All will be resurrected and stand judgment (John 5:28–29; 2 Cor 5:10). To the wicked, a loving but just God cannot grant eternal life, only the termination of existence for those who have consistently rejected divine overtures, a final darkness of non-being for all who loved darkness rather than light. The broad path of evil (Matt 7:13) pauses at God's seat of judgment but ends in eternal punishment (Matt 25:46), "eternal" signifying irreversible destruction.

1. Fudge, *Fire that Consumes*, 125–26.

Because God is just, punishment will not be "one size fits all" punishment. Rather, at the return of Christ, the one who "knows the master's will" is beaten with "many blows" while the ignorant individual is beaten with "few blows" (Luke 12:48). At the resurrection, God will judge all with fairness, with unending torment reserved for the devil, the beast, and the false prophet (Rev 20:10).[2] Mass-murderers will finally receive the retribution they avoided on earth; they can expect to be judged with severity but equitably. Punishment may be part of the destructive process itself.[3]

The Kingdom of Heaven to Gain

Stories with happy endings are always better. Thankfully, there is a bright side to destiny. The New Testament ends on a happy note! The gift of enduring life given to the faithful is conditional. It must be accepted by each of us and followed up by faithfulness to God, the evidence of the Lord's transforming presence in our lives (Eph 2:8–10). Immortality means life in God's new creation. Scripture does not teach that we "go to heaven." Rather, heaven comes down to *us*, a "New Jerusalem" adorned like a bride for her husband (Rev 21:2). This is why we pray: "Your kingdom come, your will be done on earth, as it is in heaven" (Matt 6:10). As the Robbie Seay Band sings, it will be the "God of heaven come down."[4] The

2. On a plain reading of Rev 20:10, it appears that God's justice does not rule out such a level of punishment, at least not in the case of these three.

3. Fudge, *Fire that Consumes*, 374.

4. Robbie Seay Band, "Song of Hope (Heaven Come Down)," *Give Yourself Away* (Sparrow, 2007).

Epilogue

Bible says little about what our lives will be like in the kingdom of heaven established on a new earth, but we can rest assured that our tasks will be meaningful and our joy complete.

A Final Word

And so we come to the end of this study. We've been reminded that our God of holy love will always do what is right and what is fair. That is God's nature. God is not a sadist, intent on tormenting individuals throughout eternity, nor will God force people to live in Heaven who have no desire to do so.

God has done absolutely everything possible to help us understand the depths of divine love! At great cost, Jesus came to earth and gave his life in order to reconcile us to God. We are mortal, chained by our sin, but God longs to forgive us and to break the chains in two, filling us with love for others and hope for the future. Except for those alive at Christ's return, death comes to all others, but resurrection will—for followers of Christ—inaugurate life without end in God's new creation. Now *that* is good news, indeed!

For Further Reading

These resources delve deeper into questions raised in *The Dark Side of Destiny*. This list is meant to provoke further reflection and should not necessarily be considered an endorsement by Dr. Crofford of the views of the authors.

Conditional Immortality and Eternal Conscious Torment

Fudge, William Edward, and Peterson, Robert A. *Two Views of Hell: A Biblical and Theological Dialogue.* Downer's Grove, IL: InterVarsity, 2000.

Fudge, William Edward. *The Fire that Consumes: A Biblical and Historical Study of the Doctrine of Final Punishment.* 3rd ed. Eugene, OR: Cascade Books, 2011.

———. "The Fire that Consumes." Lecture video. Online: http://www.youtube.com/watch?v=oHUP pmbTOV4.

———. *Hell: A Final Word: The Surprising Things I Found in the Bible.* Abilene, TX: Leafwood, 2012.

Resurrection

Wright, N. T. *The Resurrection of the Son of God*. Minneapolis: Fortress; London: SPCK, 2003.

What Is a Human Being?

Robinson, Howard. "Dualism." *Stanford Encyclopedia of Philosophy*. Winter 2012. Online: http://plato.stanford.edu/entries/dualism/.

Green, Joel B. *Body, Soul, and Human Life: The Nature of Humanity in the Bible*. Grand Rapids: Baker Academic, 2008.

Universalism

Moltmann, Jürgen. *Son of Righteousness, Arise!: God's Future for Humanity and the Earth*. Minneapolis: Fortress, 2010.

Wilson, Bob. "A Short Bible Case for Universalism." The Evangelical Universalist. Online: http://www.evangelicaluniversalist.com/forum/viewtopic.php?f=30&t=150.

Purgatory

Salza, John. *The Biblical Basis for Purgatory*. Charlotte, NC: Saint Benedict Press, 2009.

Schwarz, Hans. *Eschatology*. Grand Rapids: Eerdmans, 2000. See especially ch. 6, "Controversial Areas of Eschatological Hopes."

Bibliography

Books

Baker, Frank, editor. *The Works of John Wesley*.
  Bicentennial ed. 35 vols. (projected). Nashville:
  Abingdon, 1984–.
Bell, Rob. *Love Wins: A Book about Heaven, Hell, and
  the Fate of Every Person Who Ever Lived*. New York:
  HarperCollins, 2011.
Bruce, F. F. *The Hard Sayings of Jesus*. Downer's Grove,
  IL: InterVarsity, 1983.
Carson, D. A. *The Gospel according to John*. Pillar New
  Testament Commentary Series. Grand Rapids:
  Eerdmans; Leicester, UK: Apollos, 1991.
Collins, Kenneth. *The Theology of John Wesley: Holy Love
  and the Shape of Grace. Nashville:* Abingdon, 2007.
Crockett, William, editor. *Four Views on Hell*. Grand
  Rapids: Zondervan, 1992.
Dunning, H. Ray, editor. *The Second Coming: A Wesleyan
  Approach to the Doctrine of Last Things*. Kansas City,
  MS: Beacon Hill, 1995.
Ellis, E. Earle. *The Gospel of Luke*. New Century Bible
  Commentaries. 1974. Reprint, Grand Rapids:
  Eerdmans; London: Marshall, Morgan, & Scott,
  1987.

Fudge, William Edward. *The Fire that Consumes: A Biblical and Historical Study of the Doctrine of Final Punishment.* 3rd ed. Eugene, OR: Cascade Books, 2011.

Grider, J. Kenneth. *A Wesleyan-Holiness Theology.* Kansas City, MS: Beacon Hill, 1994.

Grider, J. Kenneth, et al., editors. *Beacon Dictionary of Theology.* Kansas City, MS: Beacon Hill, 1983.

Lewis, C. S. *The Great Divorce.* New York: MacMillan, 1946.

Manual of the Church of the Nazarene (2009–2013). Kansas City, MO: Nazarene Publishing House, 2009. Online: http://nazarene.org/files/docs/Manual2009-2013.pdf.

McNeill, John T., editor. *Calvin: Institutes of the Christian Religion.* 2 vols. Louisville: Westminster John Knox, 1960.

Oden, Thomas C. *John Wesley's Scriptural Christianity: A Plain Exposition of His Teaching on Christian Doctrine.* Grand Rapids: Zondervan, 1994.

Pinnock, Clark H. *A Wideness in God's Mercy: The Finality of Jesus Christ in a World of Religions.* Grand Rapids: Zondervan, 1992.

Vanhoozer, Kevin. *Theological Interpretation of the Old Testament: A Book-by-Book Survey.* Grand Rapids: Baker Academic, 2008.

Wiley, H. Orton, and Paul Culbertson. *Introduction to Christian Theology.* Kansas City, MS: Beacon Hill, 1946.

Wright, N. T. *Surprised by Hope: Rethinking Heaven, the Resurrection, and the Mission of the Church.* New York: HarperOne, 2008.

Online Resources

Bracher, Dennis, editor. "The Twenty-Five Articles of Religion (Methodist)." The Voice, Christian Resource Institute. Online: http://www.crivoice.org/creed25.html.

Edwards, Jonathan. *Sinners in the Hands of an Angry God*. Preached July 8, 1741. Transcription update by Tony Capoccia, copyright © 2007. Online: http://www.biblebb.com/files/edwards/je-sinners.htm.

Hanna, Edward. "Purgatory." *The Catholic Encyclopedia*. Vol. 12. New York: Robert Appleton, 1911. Online: http://www.newadvent.org/cathen/12575a.htm.

Harper, Douglas. "Cemetery." Online Etymology Dictionary. Online: http://www.etymonline.com/index.php?term=cemetery.

Hontheim, Joseph. "Hell." *The Catholic Encyclopedia*. Vol. 7. New York: Robert Appleton, 1910. Online: http://www.newadvent.org/cathen/07207a.htm.

Lewis, Andy. "Larry King Shocks Guests with Cryogenics Revelation: 'I Wanna Be Frozen When I Die.'" *The Hollywood Reporter*, December 5, 2011. Online: http://www.hollywoodreporter.com/live-feed/larry-king-seth-macfarlane-conan-obrien-frozen-dead-269705.

"Purgatory." Catholic Answers. Online: http://www.catholic.com/tracts/purgatory.

Westminster Confession of Faith. 1646. Online: http://www.reformed.org/documents/wcf_with_proofs/index.html.

Made in the USA
Middletown, DE
26 May 2016